ANIMAL SUPERPOWERS

AMAZING ANIMAL SENSES

John Townsend

Raintree

www.raintreepublishers.co.uk
Visit our website to find out
more information about
Raintree books.

To order:
☎ Phone 0845 6044371
🖷 Fax +44 (0) 1865 312263
✉ Email myorders@raintreepublishers.co.uk

Customers from outside the UK please telephone +44 1865 312262

Raintree is an imprint of Capstone Global Library Limited,
a company incorporated in England and Wales having its
registered office at 7 Pilgrim Street, London, EC4V 6LB –
Registered company number: 6695582

Edited by Rebecca Rissman, Dan Nunn,
  and Catherine Veitch
Designed by Joanna Hinton-Malivoire
Picture research by Mica Brancic
Production by Victoria Fitzgerald
Originated by Capstone Global Library
Printed and bound in China by CTPS

ISBN 978 1 406 24119 8
16 15 14 13 12
10 9 8 7 6 5 4 3 2 1

British Library Cataloguing in Publication Data
Townsend, John
Amazing animal senses. -- (Animal superpowers)
573.8'7-dc23
A full catalogue record for this book is available from
the British Library.

Acknowledgements
We would like to thank the following for permission to
reproduce photographs: Alamy p. 27 (© Steve Bloom
Images); Corbis pp. 12 (© David A. Northcott), 16
(© DLILLC), 17 (Science Faction/© Louie Psihoyos), 22
(© Frank Lane Picture Library/Dembinsky Photo),
23 (Visuals Unlimited/ © Ken Catania), 25 (National
Geographic Society/© Paul Nicklen); Getty Images p.
4 (Ikon Images/Steve Scott); Nature Picture Library
p. 7 (Inaki Relanzon); Photoshot p. 11 (© Juniors
Tierbildarchiv); Science Photo Library pp. 9 (John
Mitchell), 13 (Steve Gschmeissner), 20 (John Devries), 26
(ANDY MURCH/VISUALS UNLIMITED, INC.); Shutterstock
pp. 5 (Vitaly Titov & Maria Sidelnikova), 6 (© Nialat), 8
(© Audrey Snider-Bell), 10 (© Jadimages), 14
(© PhotoBarmaley), 15 (© Thomas Barrat), 18 (© Andreas
Gradin), 19 (© Evgeniy Ayupov), 21 (© EcoPrint), 24
(© L. S. Luecke), 29 (© Danomyte).

Cover photograph of a bamboo snake reproduced with
permission of Shutterstock (© Jason S).

Every effort has been made to contact copyright holders
of material reproduced in this book. Any omissions will
be rectified in subsequent printings if notice is given to
the publisher.

We would like to thank Michael Bright for his invaluable
help in the preparation of this book.

Disclaimer
All the internet addresses (URLs) given in this book were
valid at the time of going to press. However, due to the
dynamic nature of the internet, some addresses may
have changed, or sites may have changed or ceased to
exist since publication. While the author and publisher
regret any inconvenience this may cause readers, no
responsibility for any such changes can be accepted by
either the author or the publisher.

Some words are shown in bold, **like this**. You can find
out what they mean by looking in the glossary.

Contents

Animals can be superheroes!

If you want to be a superhero, you need to have super senses. You have amazing senses already, but they are nothing like the super senses of some animals. Read this book to find out which animals have senses that are out of this world!

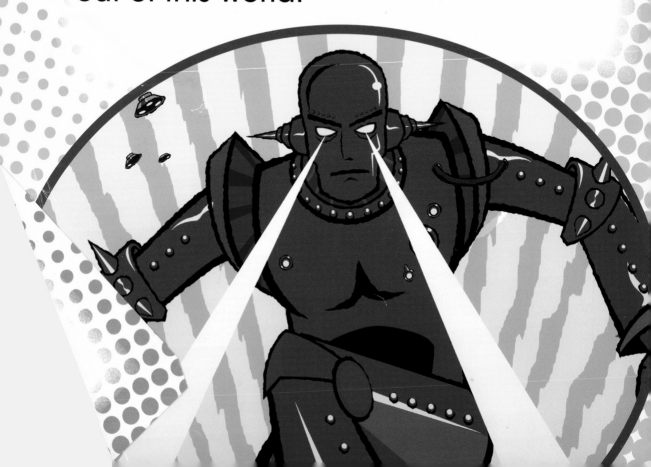

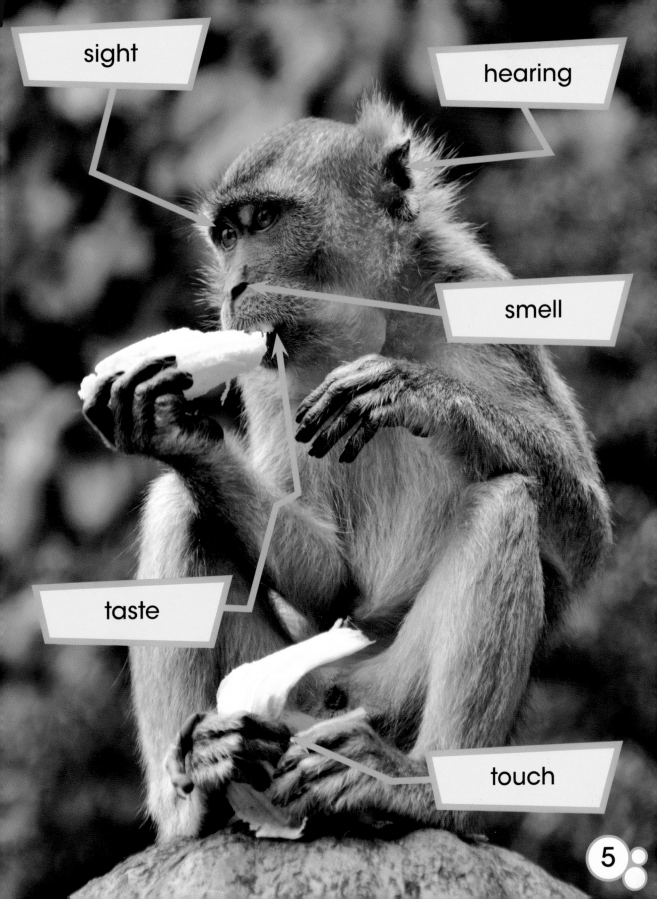

sight

hearing

smell

taste

touch

5

Super sight

Most birds of **prey** have super-sharp eyesight. Eagles can see prey up to one and a half kilometres away, and from a great height. When they dive from the sky, they keep their target in sharp **focus**.

An eagle's eyesight is four times better than a human's.

Did you know?
Bald eagles can see fish under water from high in the sky.

Special sight

Some eyes see in total darkness. Many snakes hunt at night because they can "see" heat that animals give out. Special **organs** on a snake's head work like heat goggles. They give a picture or a **thermal image** of animals' warm bodies in the darkness.

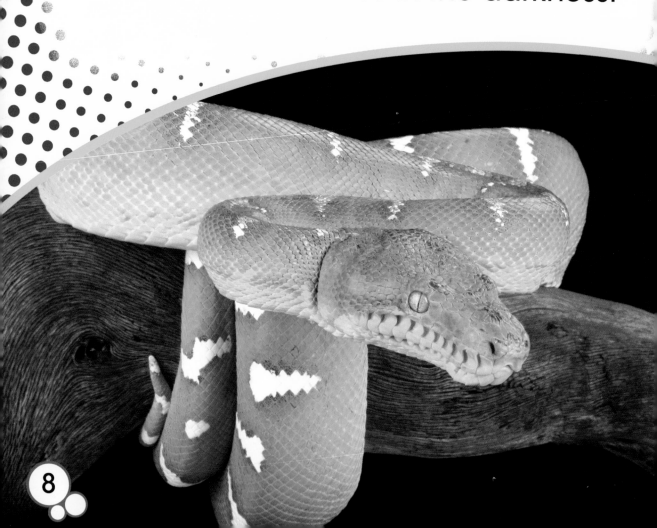

Did you know?

Rattlesnakes strike **prey** with their **venom**. Then they use their tongue to pick up its smell and find it after it has died.

prey

Super hearing

Owls have excellent eyesight, but they also have super hearing. Their large, round face acts like a bowl-shaped satellite dish and catches any sounds. If a mouse moves in the darkness, an owl can hear it from 20 metres away.

Mega hearing

Moths are never safe from night **predators**. A bat uses its amazing ears to hear silent moths over 5 metres away. Bats make clicking sounds in total darkness. They can tell where insects are from sound waves bouncing back off them.

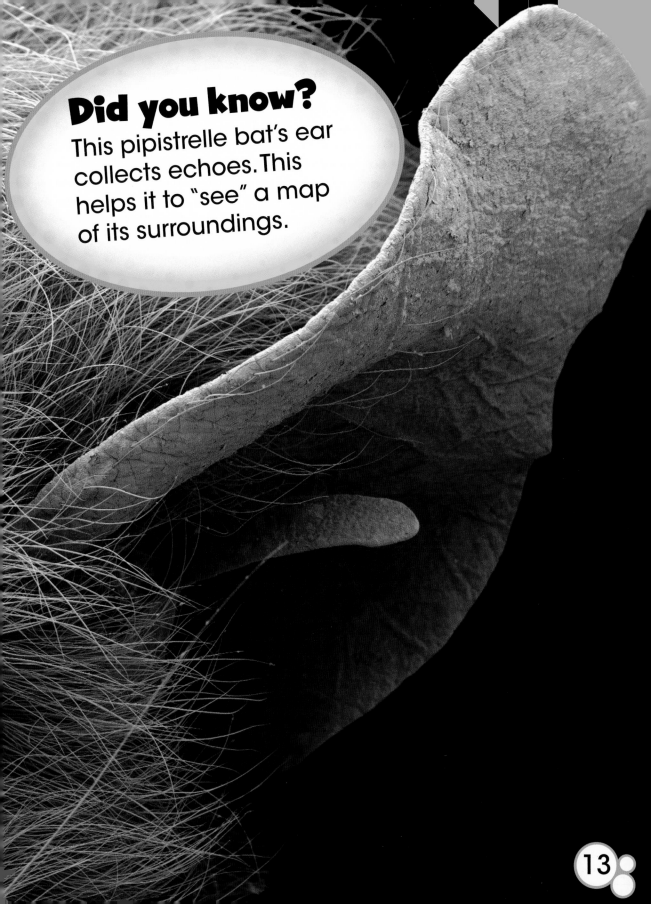

Did you know?
This pipistrelle bat's ear collects echoes. This helps it to "see" a map of its surroundings.

Super smelling

Animals often have to sniff out food over large areas. Out of all the land animals, a bear's sense of smell is one of the best. A bear's brain is smaller than a human's, but its sense of smell is five times stronger than ours.

Did you know?
A polar bear can smell **prey** from more than 30 kilometres away.

Serious sniffing

Some dogs are tracking animals, which means they are used for their excellent sense of smell. Bloodhounds may not have the sniffing power of bears, but with their brain power, they can be trained to follow **scent** trails – even ones several days old.

Bloodhounds can help the police sniff out criminals on the run.

17

Super taste

You have about 10,000 taste buds on your tongue, which help you taste food. Some animals rely on taste to survive. A catfish has about 250,000 taste buds over its whole body. They help it taste for food or feel for dangerous **predators**.

Did you know?

A fly tastes whatever it lands on through the thousands of hairs on its feet!

Mega taste

Some tongues do far more than taste food. Snakes flick out their tongues to sense chemicals and gather important information about their surroundings. A special **organ** on the roof of a snake's mouth tests the air for signs of **prey**.

forked tongue

Did you know?

This cobra knows exactly where to strike – its forked tongue can pick up information from all directions.

Super touch

In the dark you might be able to tell what objects are by touching them with your fingertips. A star-nosed mole finds food underground by feeling with its super-**sensitive** nose!

Did you know?
The mole's nose has 22 "feely fingers". They quickly track down tasty grubs in the dark.

Amazing touch

Whiskers can pick up signals in very dark places. Seals and sea lions have extra-**sensitive** whiskers packed with **sensors**. With these, they can feel **vibrations** from a fish in the dark ocean over 100 metres away.

sea lion

The monk seal's whiskers help it hunt for **prey**.

Sixth sense

Sharks have a clever way of sensing signs of movement in the water around them. Fish and other animals in the water make tiny waves of energy. Special **sensors** on the shark's head and along its body can pick up these waves.

Jelly-filled sacks around a shark's snout (nose) can sense electric signals in the water when **prey** is near.

This great white shark's sensors tell it to attack this seal.

Quiz: Spot the superhero!

Test your powers of observation and see if you can spot the superhero. You can find the answers on page 32 if you are really stuck!

1. Which of these animals has the best sense of sight?
   a) a mole
   b) a catfish
   c) an eagle

2. Which of these animals has the best sense of hearing?
   a) a snake
   b) an owl
   c) a fly

3. Which of these animals has the best sense of **scent**?
a) a bat
b) an eagle
c) a bear

4. Which of these animals has the best sense of taste?
a) a catfish
b) a shark
c) a mole

5. Which of these animals has the best sense of touch?
a) a snake
b) a mole
c) a moth

Glossary

focus adjusting the eye so something can be seen clearly

organ part of an animal's body that has a particular job to do

predator animal that hunts other animals

prey animal that is hunted by other animals for food

scent smell left behind after a person or animal has passed by

sensitive able to feel or notice very small differences, details, and sensations

sensor something that notices movement or light, and signals in response

thermal image picture formed by sensing heat energy given off by an animal or object

venom poison that is injected

vibration trembling movement

Find out more

Books

Amazing Animals (Explorers), Jinny Johnson (Kingfisher, 2012)

Animals (Starting Science), Sally Hewitt (Franklin Watts, 2010)

Reptiles, Catriona Clarke (Usborne, 2009)

Websites

http://faculty.washington.edu/chudler/amaze. html
This website has information about the amazing animal senses.

www.bbc.co.uk/nature/adaptations/Haptic_ perception#p006b9c0
Watch how seals feel their way underwater on this website.

Index

Answers: 1c, 2b, 3c, 4a, 5b.